THE NORMAN C

LIVING TOGETHER

A Play

ALAN AYCKBOURN

SAMUEL   FRENCH

LONDON
NEW YORK   TORONTO   SYDNEY   HOLLYWOOD

LIVING TOGETHER

First presented by the Library Theatre Co., Scarborough in June 1973 and subsequently by the Greenwich Theatre Company in May 1974, and in London by Michael Codron at the Globe Theatre in August 1974, with the following cast of characters:

Norman	Tom Courtenay
Tom	Michael Gambon
Sarah	Penelope Keith
Annie	Felicity Kendal
Reg	Mark Kingston
Ruth	Bridget Turner

The play directed by Eric Thompson
Setting by Alan Pickford

The action passes in the sitting-room of a Victorian vicarage-type house during a week-end in July

ACT I
    Scene 1   Saturday, 6.30 p.m.
    Scene 2   Saturday, 8 p.m.

ACT II
    Scene 1   Sunday, 9 p.m.
    Scene 2   Monday, 8 a.m.

Period – the present

ACT I

SCENE 1

The sitting-room. Saturday, 6.30 p.m.

It is a high-ceilinged Victorian room in need of redecoration. A french window leads to the garden, and a door to the rest of the house. Furnishings include a settee, easy chair, pouffe, a small table, a coffee-table, and a fireplace in front of which is a brown fur rug

As the CURTAIN *rises, Sarah, in a light summer coat and dress, is in the process of lifting a suitcase from the floor on to the table to open it. Reg enters from the garden in cap and sports jacket, carrying another bag and a large pile of magazines tied with string. He is followed by Norman, bearded in woolly hat and raincoat, carrying his own battered suitcase. Norman flings himself into the easy chair and sits grumpily. Reg puts the magazines on the table behind the settee*

Reg That's the lot. Well, come on. Where is she then? Where is she? Where's my little sister?

Sarah Ssh. Mother's resting.

Reg Oh. (*Wandering back to the window*) We ought to cut down the vegetation in the tennis court and have a game, Norman. Fancy a game?

Norman I hate tennis.

Sarah I thought you were in a hurry to go somewhere, Norman.

Norman Not at all.

Reg Yes, I thought you said you had a—librarians' conference.

Norman It's been cancelled.

Reg When?

Norman About ten seconds ago. Due to lack of interest.

Reg Funny lot these librarians. Now, where's Annie, do you know?

Sarah She's in there.

Reg Ah. (*He moves to the door*)

Sarah Wait.

Reg Why?

Sarah She's busy. Tom's in there with her, having a talk.

Reg Well, she can talk to Tom any time. I've come all the way to see her.

Sarah Wait.

Reg What made her change her mind? About going? I mean, I thought the idea was, we came down here, nursed Mother for the week-end and Annie went off somewhere and had a good time. No point in us being here now, is there? Might as well not have come. Not that I mind. Nice to see the country. Beautiful evening. No kids . . .

Sarah Where did you pack that present for Mother?

Reg What present?

Sarah The bed-jacket. The blue bed-jacket, it was wrapped in tissue. Where is it?

Reg Never set eyes on it.

Sarah (*removing a large playing board, bits of cardboard, etc. from the case*) What's all this you've packed?

Reg My game.

Sarah Why did you want to bring it down here?

Reg I thought there might be someone around, we could try it out. I've invented it, I want to try it out. I mean, the kids won't play it with me, you won't play it with me—how do I know if it works if no-one'll play it? Norman can play.

Norman Eh?

Sarah I should think Norman's had enough of games, haven't you, Norman?

Reg Eh?

Sarah Anyway, Norman's going in a minute, aren't you, Norman?

Reg What's all this? What's going on between you two?

Sarah I'll tell you later.

Reg (*putting the game on the coffee-table*) Oh, yes . . . ? If you're planning an affair, let me know and I'll book my holiday.

Sarah (*giving up her search*) Oh well, that's that. No present for Mother. You've forgotten to pack it. Oh well, I'll give her these magazines and tell her we'll send the bed-jacket on to her. It took me ages to make that. If you knew how I hated knitting.

Reg We do. We know. We sat round all winter watching her with bated breath. One dropped stitch and you could say good-bye to your supper . . . Hey, one of my little men is missing.

Sarah Oh, my God.

Reg I've lost my Chief Superintendent. Is he at the bottom of the suitcase? (*He goes to look in the suitcase*)

Sarah I have no idea. Our house is littered with little men.

Reg And she's complaining. (*He chuckles*)

Sarah You're very pensive, Norman.

Norman I'm wondering which is the cleanest and quickest way to finish myself off.

Reg Well, don't get married. That's long and messy. Ah-ha, here he is. (*He holds up a small cardboard figure on a base which he has rescued from the suitcase*) The Chief Superintendent in person. Nearly had a nasty accident. Got himself tangled up in a nasty web of blue woolly . . . oh.

Sarah Give that to me. (*She retrieves her bed-jacket from Reg*)

Reg (*putting the figure with the game*) It was there all the time. Just needed a good copper to find it.

Sarah Would you mind taking these upstairs.

Reg (*taking the suitcases*) My pleasure. (*He moves to the door whistling*)

Sarah And don't wake Mother if she's dozing.

Reg I'll go and say hallo to Annie first.

Sarah I've told you, she's . . .

Reg I haven't seen her for three months. She's my sister. I want to say hallo.

Sarah She and Tom are . . .

Reg Oh, to blazes with Tom.

Reg goes out to the house, whistling

Sarah (*turning her attention to Norman*) It's no good sitting there looking sorry for yourself. I'm appalled at you, I really am.

Norman (*jeering*) Jealous?

Sarah Don't be disgusting. Annie of all people. How could you? What on earth made you do it?

Norman I haven't done anything.

Sarah Annie has told me everything.

Norman Has she? And what could she possibly tell you?

Sarah About you two—last Christmas. In this house. With your wife ill upstairs—rolling about with her sister on this very rug.

Norman Oh—that—that was just festive fun.

Sarah And if that isn't enough, planning to sneak off with her for some sordid week-end.

Norman There's nothing sordid about East Grinstead. She wanted to come. I wanted to go. Don't you see? It would have been something different for her—exciting. And for me. She's stuck here, all on her own, day after day looking after that old sabre-toothed bat upstairs . . .

Sarah Will you not refer to Mother like that.

Norman Oh, come on. She's not your mother, she's not my mother. She's a mother-in-law. Fair game. I'll call her what I like. You ought to hear what Annie calls her sometimes. Anyway, we happen to love each other. Me and Annie, that is, not me and mother-in-law.

Sarah Don't be ridiculous. You're married to Ruth.

Norman What's that got to do with it?

Sarah And Annie, I may remind you, has her fiancé to consider.

Norman (*scornfully*) Her who?

Sarah Her—well—her whatever she calls him—Tom.

Norman Tom.

Sarah Yes. He may not be ideal in many ways but beggars can't be choosers . . .

Norman She's not a beggar.

Sarah Maybe not. But it would be stupid to make out she had a very wide choice as regards a possible husband. She's not—well . . .

Norman She's beautiful.

Sarah I'm not going to argue. Certainly no-one could describe her as beautiful. I'll admit she has a great deal of . . .

Norman Anybody I love is automatically beautiful.

Sarah Oh, Norman, don't be ridiculous.

Norman Have you never felt that way? Perhaps you've never been in love. Maybe that's your trouble. Was Reg never beautiful in your eyes?

Sarah I'm not discussing my private life . . .

Norman You're being free enough with mine, aren't you?

Sarah Yours doesn't happen to be particularly private, does it? It happens to involve about half a dozen people. You, Annie, Ruth, Tom, Reg, me and Mother.

Norman I've never asked Mother for a week-end anywhere. (*Moving to the window*) Look at that cat up there. He's still up that tree. Tom was trying to get it down. He can't be much of a vet. What sort of a vet are you, when you terrify your patients into climbing trees? Something wrong with his basket-side manner, I'd say. What do you say, Sarah? Would you say you were a fulfilled person?

Sarah I don't know what you mean.

Norman Are you happy then?

Sarah Yes—mostly. Occasionally. Now and then. I don't know. I don't have time to think about it. When you've a family like mine you're too busy . . .

Norman You're very lucky. I can't say Ruth and I are happy.

Sarah Well, I'm not surprised if you . . . (*Checking herself*) She's not the easiest person I admit.

Norman No.

Sarah Then neither are you.

Norman I'm very warm and affectionate, you know.

Sarah Yes. So are dogs. But they don't make particularly good husbands.

Norman Ah well, like me, they invariably marry—lady dogs. Perhaps I should leave her.

Sarah Yes, do. Please do. I think it would be better for both of you. But for heaven's sake, clear off completely and whatever you do, stop pestering Annie. She doesn't want you, not really.

Norman I supposed you talked her out of going away with me.

Sarah I didn't need to. She'd already made up her own mind. I certainly didn't encourage her . . . I must go up and see Mother.

Norman It was going to be a lovely time. We were going to meet behind the post office in the village at seven o'clock and steal away on the bus to our hotel. Forget everything, everybody, just lie anonymously in each other's arms. Just for a day.

Sarah We'd still be here when you came back.

Norman I feel terribly depressed.

Sarah Serve you right.

Norman You haven't told Tom, have you?

Sarah That's up to Annie. Nothing to do with me.

Norman Nothing? You only talked her out of going.

Sarah I have already said, I did no such thing. It was Annie's decision.

Norman I hope she doesn't tell Tom.

Sarah Why?

Norman It'd upset him.

Sarah It's a bit late to consider his feelings now, isn't it? Having tried to steal Annie from under his nose.

Norman I wasn't stealing her, I was borrowing her. For the week-end.

Sarah Make her sound like one of your library books.
Norman She was borrowing me, too. It was mutual. It was a friendly loan. We never intended to upset anybody. We both agreed. That was the joy of it, don't you see? Nobody need ever have known. If Annie hadn't gone and told you—nobody.
Sarah Oh, well. It's up to Annie if she wants to tell Tom. Nothing to do with me. (*She tries to lift the magazine pile*) Oh, these are far too heavy, I'll get Reg to take them up later. Now, for goodness' sake, Norman, pull yourself together and go home to Ruth.
Norman Why did you stop her going, Sarah? Be honest. Why?
Sarah I've told you why . . .

Sarah goes out to the house with the bed-jacket

Norman (*mournfully*) I really am very depressed. (*He mooches about. He pulls a magazine from the pile and flips through it. Something catches his eye and he starts reading. After a moment, he starts to laugh. He finds the article increasingly hysterical*)

Annie comes in. She stares at him

Annie Norman. (*She closes the door*)
Norman (*springing up guiltily*) Oh. Hallo, Annie.
Annie You all right?
Norman Yes, I was just trying to cheer myself up.
Annie Looks like you've succeeded.
Norman No.
Annie Norman, I'm awfully sorry. Really. I expect Sarah's told you.
Norman She said you'd thought better of it.
Annie Yes. I feel dreadful after all the trouble you've taken. Booking East Grinstead and things. It's just . . .
Norman It's all right. (*Pause*) Oh, why did you let her talk you out of it.
Annie I didn't.
Norman Don't tell me you'd have changed your mind if she hadn't . . .
Annie Things were getting very complicated, you see. I mean, when we were planning it, last Christmas and on the phone and things—well—it was simple then, wasn't it? It was easy just to forget about Ruth and —Tom and so on. Not that Tom's all that important but after all, you are married to Ruth and she is my sister, even if I'm not all that fond of her, but I don't think I'm very good at pretending for very long. Sarah got it out of me in no time.
Norman Yes. She would.
Annie And I don't think I'd have been much fun to be with, anyway. I'd have been worrying all the time. Are you furious with me?
Norman No.
Annie Oh, Norman, you look so miserable. (*Kneeling on the rug*) I am sorry.
Norman Don't . . .

Annie What?

Norman Don't kneel on that rug if you don't mind. It reminds me.

Annie Oh, yes. Our rug. (*She gives a short giggle*) I got the fire-tongs mended.

Norman Oh, yes.

Annie Tom fixed them.

Norman Oh. What does he have to say about all this?

Annie Tom? I don't think he knows.

Norman He doesn't?

Annie I haven't told him.

Norman Oh.

Annie Sarah might.

Norman I bet she will. She said she won't. But she will. She'll be dropping big circular hints. She's never kept a secret in her life . . .

Annie She'll have to chalk it up in huge letters. You know, I'm really very fond of Tom but he really is terribly heavy going: Like running uphill in roller skates. Not like you. "Beautiful sunset, isn't it, Tom?" "Um." Everything's um. Probably works a treat when he's stamping out swine fever, but it's pretty boring over dinner. "Do you like the wine, Tom?" "Um." Honestly, Norman?

Norman Mmm? I mean, yes.

Annie What are you going to tell Ruth?

Norman What I was going to tell her anyway. I've been on a conference.

Annie Which finished early?

Norman Something like that. We ran out of things to talk about. What does it matter. She won't care. She probably thinks I'm in the attic mending the roof.

Annie I didn't know assistant librarians had conferences.

Norman Everybody has conferences.

Annie You'll be able to get back all right?

Norman Yes.

Annie Oh dear . . .

Norman What?

Annie You look so limp. Like an old tea towel.

Annie impulsively leans forward to kiss him on the cheek

Reg enters

Annie jumps away and straightens the corner of the rug

Reg (*standing awkwardly*) Er—hallo again. Excuse me, just came in for something. (*He stands uncertainly*)

Norman What?

Reg What? Yes—what? Er . . . (*He picks up the waste-paper basket from behind the settee table*) Ah. This is it. This is it. Thank you. Carry on.

Reg goes out

Norman Do you ever get the feeling you're being watched? Sarah's secret agent. Our days together are numbered.

Annie So are our minutes.

Norman (*rising and going to the window*) Come on then.

Annie What?

Norman It's now or never. What do you say?

Annie What is?

Norman We can be through the gap in the hedge and half-way down the lane before they realize we've gone.

Annie (*drawing back*) Oh, Norman . . .

Norman What's to stop us? I love you—you love me—we're in love. We should be together. It's right. Believe me, it's right. We have right on our side.

Annie (*doubtfully*) Well . . .

Norman Don't you see, we're not alone? We've got the whole tradition of history behind us. We're not the first lovers who've ever done this—stood up to the whole establishment and said to hell with the *status quo*, we don't care what's meant to be, we mean this to be. Us. And there's nothing can stand in our way, you know. Not if you think about it. What is there to stop us?

Annie Mother's pills . . .

Norman Eh?

Annie I can't just rush away. I have to explain to them about Mother's pills.

Norman (*passionately*) My God! The course of true love shattered not by the furies, not by the fates but by Mother's bleeding pills.

Annie Not only that.

Norman It's all right. That's enough to be getting on with. Don't swamp me with any more overwhelming arguments. Dear Juliet, my shoelace has come undone, I cannot join you in the tomb. Love, Romeo. Dear Tristan, owing to a sudden tax demand . . .

Annie All right, Norman, all right.

Pause. Norman simmers down

Norman That's it then.

Annie Yes. That's it.

Norman Oh.

A pause

Tom enters from the house

Tom Ah.

Norman Gone. All gone.

Tom Glad I've caught you.

Norman Oh, it's Tom. Hallo, Tom. (*He shakes Tom's hand*) Haven't seen you for ages. How are you?

Tom Fine. Just been talking to you in the garden, haven't I?

Norman Oh, yes. I forgot. I think it was me.

Tom Don't quite follow you.

Norman It was probably me. On the other hand it could have been you.

Tom Me what?

Norman Talking to yourself.

Annie Norman . . .

Tom Hang on, I'm getting confused here.

Norman How unusual.

Annie Norman . . .

Norman Anyway, my mistake.

Tom (*doubtful*) Yes. I—wanted a word with you.

Annie (*moving to the door*) I'll get on out there.

Tom No. Hang on. Hang on a second, Annie. Would you mind.

Annie sits on the settee

Norman Recriminations. Here they come. (*He sits in the easy chair*)

Tom Um?

Norman Nothing.

Tom The point is . . . (*He pauses uncertainly and wanders to the window*) Is that cat still up that tree, by the way?

Norman Hanging on grimly. As we all are.

Tom I suppose he'll come down eventually . . . The point is, something seems to be going on which I've not been let into.

Norman Has it?

Tom Apparently. Sarah was talking about something.

Norman (*to Annie*) What did I tell you?

Tom What?

Norman Come on, let's have it. What did she say?

Tom That's it, you see. I couldn't make it out.

Norman You couldn't?

Tom Not really.

Norman Oh—good.

Annie Would you both like something to drink?

Tom Thought perhaps you could enlighten me.

Norman Yes, please. A great deal.

Annie I'll see what we've got.

Annie goes out

Tom Annie's a bit angry with me.

Norman Is she?

Tom Yes. You know she was planning to go away this week-end?

Norman Yes.

Tom Well, reading between the lines, I think she was rather hoping that old you-know-who would go with her.

Norman Who?

Tom Me.

Norman You?

Tom Yes.

Norman She asked you?

Tom Very obliquely.

Norman Must have been.

Tom Now she's not going. And it seems to be my fault.

Norman It is.

Tom You think so?

Norman Definitely. If she's not going away, it's entirely due to you.

Tom Yes, I was afraid of that. The question is, how do I get myself out of the dog's kennel and back in the pantry.

Norman I beg your pardon?

Tom Back in her good books.

Norman Very difficult.

Tom Is it?

Norman Want my opinion?

Tom I'd welcome it.

Norman I think you've given her too much. I think she's in danger of being spoilt. She's taking you for granted.

Tom Really?

Norman She's taking everyone for granted. What she needs is a bit of the old boot.

Tom Boot?

Norman Bit of the rough stuff.

Tom Oh, come on. Boot? Come on . . .

Norman Metaphorical.

Tom Oh, metaphorical boot. What's that exactly?

Norman Tell her she's damned lucky to have you around. And the next time she's planning holidays for two, she can come and ask you politely if you'd like to come. If you don't watch it, she'll walk all over you. Couple of sharp words, she'll jump. Tell her she looks a mess. If she wants to be seen around with you in future, she'd better smarten up her ideas. She looks like something that's fallen off a post van. I mean, what the hell right has she to promise something and then let you down at the last minute? It would serve her right if you belted her one and gave her rabies. That's my opinion. (*He pauses breathless*)

Tom (*very bewildered*) Is it?

Norman She'd respect you for that.

Tom Well, I'll bear it in mind but . . .

Annie enters with three wineglasses, three bottles of wine tucked under her arms, and a corkscrew. She is having difficulty

Annie It'll have to be the home-made stuff.

Tom (*leaping up*) Oh, let me . . . (*He takes a bottle which appears to be slipping from under her arm*)

Annie Thanks.

Tom catches Norman's eye. Norman shakes his head disapprovingly. Tom stares at the bottle he is holding. Annie stands waiting for Tom to take the other bottles from her. Instead, Tom puts his bottle back in her arms and sits on the settee

Oh, thank you so much. That's a great help. Don't put yourselves out, will you.

Norman No.

Tom No.

Annie (*putting the things on the settee table*) What's got into you two?

Norman Nothing.

Tom No.

Annie Well, if you want a drink, you can damn well open them. (*She sits on the settee*)

Tom hesitates and finally gets up. Norman clucks disapprovingly

Tom Well—parsnip or dandelion?

Norman We have a choice?

Tom Both last year's. I think I'd recommend the parsnip. It's slightly mellower. The dandelion's rather lethal. Oh, and there's some carrot.

Annie Don't touch the dandelion—it's a killer. I didn't mean to bring it in.

Tom Parsnip then?

Norman Dandelion.

Tom You sure?

Norman Positive.

Tom Oh well . . . (*He starts to open the bottles*)

Annie I have a feeling there's trouble brewing in the dining-room. I passed the door just now and Reg and Sarah seemed to be limbering up.

Norman That should set the seal on the week-end.

Annie As long as Mother doesn't hear them.

Tom No, we don't want her upset.

Annie It won't upset her. She'll insist on being carried downstairs to be in at the kill. There's nothing she likes better than a good row.

Norman In the old days she used to start them all.

Annie She and Sarah. She really loathed Sarah.

Norman Even Mother-in-law has her good side.

Annie Tom's frightened to go up there, aren't you?

Tom Well . . .

Annie She thinks he's a doctor.

Tom Can't get it through to her I'm a vet. She insists I take her pulse, listen to her—chest and other things. Very embarrassing.

Norman She's mad for the feel of manly hands. She knows what she's doing, don't worry.

Tom Yes, I think she does. (*Examining a glassful of wine*) Better just try this first. (*He samples it*)

Annie (*loudly in Norman's direction*) What's it like, Tom?

Tom Um . . . (*He ponders*)

Annie (*raising her eyebrows to heaven, softly*) Um . . .

Tom (*bringing a glass to Annie*) Not bad, not bad, here—parsnip.
Annie Thanks.
Tom (*to Norman*) Dandelion.
Norman Ta.
Annie (*examining her glass*) It's clearer than usual.
Tom Yes.
Annie It's usually like soup. You have to filter it through your front teeth.
Norman (*raising his glass by way of a toast*) Well. Um . . .
Annie (*giggling*) Um . . .
Tom Yes. Cheers. (*Pause*) Um—you know, I've been thinking. (*He sits on the settee*) What would have been rather nice. Too late now—but another year. Supposing there is another year that is . . .
Norman Why? Are you planning to bring the world to an end shortly?
Tom No, no.
Norman This is very potent.
Annie Very. Brewed by Mother. Last thing she did before she was ill.
Norman She knows her spells.
Tom What would have been rather nice . . .
Norman (*finding a bit in his glass*) Ah.
Annie What is it?
Norman Bit of cork. Or a toad's leg.
Tom What would have been awfully nice is if we'd all three gone. Don't you think.

Annie and Norman stare at him

I mean, we all get on well. It would have been rather fun . . .
Norman I beg your pardon?
Tom If Annie and you and I had all gone way together on her week-end.
Norman (*highly amused*) Oh, my God. (*Rising and crossing to the wine*) More wine . . .
Tom Single rooms, of course.
Norman (*taking up the bottle of dandelion wine and returning to his chair*) Oh, yes, single rooms.
Tom I didn't mean anything like that.
Norman (*laughing openly*) No. Nothing like that.
Tom What's funny?
Norman (*helplessly*) Nothing.
Annie (*angry*) Oh, Tom, honestly.
Tom Eh?
Annie You're so dim. You're so completely and utterly dismally dim.
Tom What?
Annie You make me mad, you're so stupid. You're boring, slow-witted, dull and utterly stupid.
Tom (*slightly injured, no more*) What have I said now? What have I said now?
Norman Now's the time to knock her down.
Annie I'm fed up with both of you. You've ruined my week-end.
Tom All I said was . . .

Annie (*yelling*) I heard what you said. Thank you very much. I heard what you said.

Norman is still laughing, highly amused by this

And, Norman, just shut up.

Norman does so. A silence

Tom Well . . .

Annie (*muttering*) Stupid men . . .

A crash and a scream from Sarah is heard from the dining-room

Norman Meanwhile, in the dining-room, the first shots are being fired in anger.

Annie (*leaping up*) Oh, no . . . (*Hurrying to the door*) I wish you'd all go away, all of you, and leave me in peace.

Annie goes out leaving her glass on the table

Tom She's like a tiger when she's roused, isn't she?

Norman I've never met a tiger socially, I wouldn't know.

Tom Something's got into her, you know. I think that holiday meant more to her than she's letting on.

Norman Yes, I'm beginning to think that. (*Proffering the bottle*) *Plus de vin?*

Tom No, no. Spoil my dinner. You'd better be careful or you'll finish up here for the night.

Norman That's a point. (*He pours himself another*)

Tom moves to the window

Tom (*calling*) Pussy, pussy. Down, puss. Come down, puss. Pussy, pussy. I wish they'd given the animal a name. I really do.

Norman pours another glass

I should go easy on that. I had a very unpleasant side reaction.

Norman It doesn't show.

Tom Well, I think I'll go and see if I can pour oil on things. Not going immediately, are you?

Norman Not immediately.

Tom Right.

Tom goes out

Norman rises to his feet and finds already he is a bit unsteady. He goes to the window

Norman (*French pronunciation*) Dan-de-lion. (*At the window; calling*) You stay up there, mate. If you come down, he'll only want paying.

Tom returns with his glass

Tom Oh, Lord . . .

Norman Back again?

Tom I think I'll keep out of there for a second. The room's positively knee. deep in home truths—if you know what I mean.

Norman Splendid.

Tom That and biscuits.

Norman Biscuits?

Tom Yes, they seem to have been throwing biscuits around. Water biscuits.

Norman You can do someone a nasty injury with a water biscuit . . .

Annie appears fleetingly in the doorway with a dustpan and brush

Annie All hell's been let loose in there.

Annie goes

Tom Do you need a . . . (*He realizes she has gone*)

Pause. Tom wanders to the table and discovers Reg's game

Tom (*examining it*) What's all this? Looks like another of Reg's home-made games. Looks even more complicated than usual. I better keep out of the way if he decides to play it. Reg gets rather irritated with me. Always very slow on getting the hang of the rules. (*Slight pause*) Norman. Frankly—answer me something.

Norman Mmm?

Tom Do you think I'm dim and dismal? I think that's what she said. Yes, that was it. Dim and dismal and stupid. Do I come across as that?

Norman Um—no. I'd say—you had the good fortune to be born without a single suspicious or malicious thought in your head.

Tom Oh, I don't know.

Norman Yes. Yes, true. And that can get you in a lot of trouble. Because you're more or less on your own, you see. And whenever people feel like taking a really good swing at something, to relieve their feelings, you come in extremely handy. No come back, you see.

Tom I haven't noticed people doing that. You've got the wrong chap.

Norman (*waving a fist in the air*) You've got to develop a come-back. (*Studying Tom*) I mean, looking at you standing there, I don't think there's anyone in there at all. You're somewhere else. That's remote control, all that lot.

Tom That stuff's beginning to tell. I warned you about the dandelion.

Norman Don't worry about a thing.

Tom Well, I'd better go and see if the dining-room's cooled off a bit. I'll take them in a bottle. (*He takes one*)

Norman Want a tip?

Tom What?

Norman Go in there laughing.

Tom Laughing?

Norman There's nothing they like better in this family than a good laugh.
Go on. Bring an atmosphere of merriment into the room. (*He gives
a false laugh*)
Tom (*copying Norman*) All right. I'll try it. You're a good chap, Norman,
you know. A very good chap.
Norman Thank you.
Tom I'm sorry you're having to dash away. To your—conference. Pity
you're not staying. You brighten the place up a bit. Pity. Cheerio.
Norman Cheerio.

Tom goes out

Norman laughs

Tom appears at the door, laughs, and goes

*Norman goes to the door and laughs. Tom is heard laughing, off. Norman
closes the door, laughing. He finds the gramophone under the occasional table,
puts it on the table, opens it, takes the record off the turntable and reads the
label, hums a line from "Girls were made to Love and Kiss". He replaces the
record. Winds the gramophone up, and starts the record. He does a dance to
the music and sings as the vocal starts. At one point he opens the door and
"sings out" to the corridor. He returns, singing, puts his glass on the floor
below the rug, and finally collapses on the rug*

Here's to you, Tom, old boy. Here's to the lot of you.

He sings louder, as—

the Curtain *falls*

Scene 2

The same. Saturday, 8 p.m.

*Norman is asleep, on the rug, with bottles and a glass beside him. Reg and
Tom enter from the house without seeing him*

Reg . . . no, no. You say to me, who's there, you see . . .
Tom Oh, it's me who says that. I see. All right. Who's there?
Reg Start again. Knock knock.
Tom Come in—I mean, who's there?
Reg Vet.
Tom Vet?
Reg No. You say, vet who?
Tom Vet who, sorry. Come in—who's there—vet who.
Reg There's no "come in". Start again.
Tom Right-ho. Knock knock.

Reg Who's there—no. I should have started it. Knock knock.

Tom Who's there?

Reg Vet.

Tom Vet who?

Reg Vet kind of door is this, you can't afford a bell. (*He laughs*)

Tom Yes, I think I've got it now—try it again.

Reg That's it.

Tom Oh, is it? Quite simple, really.

Reg Yes . . . (*Seeing Norman*) Good God! Look at that.

Tom Oh. It's Norman. (*They move to him*) Is he all right?

Reg Norman! Norman! (*No response*) He's out like a light.

Tom I thought he'd gone.

Reg So did everybody. When he finally stopped singing and peace descended over the fruit and cream, I thought we'd lost him. Sarah's going to be pleased.

Tom Ought we to move him?

Reg Well, he's not in anybody's way. Oy . . . (*He kicks Norman*)

Norman grunts

(*Moving away*) Leave him, I think. Oh, I'm starving after that meal. Salad. I can't bear salad. It grows while you're eating it, you know. Have you noticed. You start one side of your plate and by the time you've got to the other, there's a fresh crop of lettuce taken root and sprouted up. You have to start again. And it still doesn't fill you. You finish up exhausted and hungry. The only thing that keeps me going when I'm eating a salad is the hope that somebody might have thought it was my birthday and hidden something to eat under all the vegetation. But they never do. A sardine if you're lucky.

Tom (*still with Norman*) He's still breathing.

Reg I should hope so. He's enough trouble as he is without dying on us. The problem with this house is there's no television.

Tom It's very shallow breathing. Do you think I should take his hat off?

Reg He doesn't breathe through the top of his head, does he? Oh I don't know, he might do knowing Norman. (*Bending over him*) If I were you, I'd pull it down over his face—like this. (*He does so*) There you are, great improvement.

Tom It's the dandelion, you see. Look at that, he's had nearly a bottle. Drowning his sorrows, I suspect.

Reg Sorrows?

Tom Well, I was talking to him earlier. He was obviously very disturbed. Depressed . . .

Reg Was he? Well . . .

Tom Don't know why, I'm sure. You know something, though, I've got a theory there's probably a woman at the back of it. Man gets drunk like this, it's generally a woman. Ruth, do you think?

Reg Possibly. Possibly . . .

Tom Perhaps Sarah would know. She usually keeps her ear close to the ground. Better ask her.

Reg (*hastily*) No, I wouldn't Tom, really.

Tom No?

Reg No. The point is, Sarah did whisper something to me, as a matter of fact. Norman mentioned something to her. Confidentially.

Tom Oh. Did he? Anything we can do to help? I mean, he's a good chap. Pity to see him like this.

Reg Well apparently, he had something lined up for tonight, you see.

Tom Yes, his Annual Librarians' Conference. He told me. He'll have missed that now, won't he?

Reg No, it was something else, you see. He'd apparently lined up a bit on the side.

Tim A bit on the side?

Reg Oh, you know Norman. Any pretty girl—he's away.

Tom Oh, I see. And she's let him down?

Reg Apparently.

Tom I see. Any idea who she is?

Reg No. No. None at all.

Tom Oh. Pity. I mean, it might have been worth almost trying to contact her. Seeing if we couldn't patch things up. Mind you, if she could see him now, she'd probably feel she'd made the right decision.

Annie comes in from the house

Annie I have never known a house where you can have a blazing row over who's going to make the coffee . . . (*Seeing Norman*) Oh, no! Norman! What's the matter with him?

Reg He's taken an overdose.

Annie An overdose? Of what? (*Trying to revive Norman*) Norman— Norman.

Tom Of dandelion wine.

Annie What?

Tom He's had too much of it, that's all.

Annie You mean, he's just drunk?

Reg Give her a prize.

Annie Norman, you idiot—get up. (*She kicks him*)

Norman (*sleepily*) Hallo.

Annie Oh, look at him, he's disgusting. Sarah'll be delighted to see him. I thought he'd gone home.

Tom No, well—actually—we were just saying, he's probably like this because of his bit on the side.

Annie Bit on the side?

Reg Yes, well, we don't want to go into all that now, Tom.

Annie What bit on the side?

Tom Oh, you know Norman. Any pretty girl. He'd got some bit on the side lined up for the week-end. She went and ditched him.

Annie Norman told you that?

Reg No.

Tom You've just said he did.

Reg Yes, well he did, but . . .

Tom Yes, he did.

Annie He did. (*Kicking Norman*) Get up, you drunken slob.

Norman (*Without waking up*) Hallo.

Reg (*sitting on the pouffe*) I wouldn't do too much of that, Annie.

Annie Wouldn't you. I would. (*She kicks him again*)

Tom Sorry. I didn't mean to shock you. Did I shock you, telling you that?

Annie Yes.

Tom Oh. Sorry. Anyway, that's why he's drunk. He's been let down by . . .

Annie By his bit on the side? Well, lucky him.

Tom wanders to the window. Annie glares at Reg who whistles nonchalantly. Annie wanders to sit, passing Reg who moves his leg out of her way as she passes

Tom He's still up there. The cat. Think he's staging some sort of protest.

Annie Oh, forget the damn cat.

Tom Think I'll switch on the outside lights, if you don't mind. Might encourage him down, when it gets dark.

Tom goes out to the garden for a second, and an exterior light comes on

Reg Sarah making the coffee, is she?

Annie She was fighting for the privilege. Literally.

Tom returns

Tom Lovely evening. Going to be quite a sunset. Really quite something. You know, I don't think I altogether got the point of that vet joke.

Reg Never mind, never mind.

Annie You haven't been telling him jokes again?

Reg I tried my best.

Annie You never learn, do you? And no more rows between you and Sarah, please.

Reg I didn't so anything. Just standing there, she flung this tin of biscuits at me—oh, don't talk about biscuits, I'm starving. (*He takes two magazines from the pile*)

Annie She probably had good cause.

Reg Nonsense.

Annie Must remember to give Mother her medicine in fifteen minutes.

Tom It's on a night like this, you know, one could really fancy going out and sleeping under the stars. Used to do that when I was at college.

Reg Didn't it have a roof then? (*He sits in the easy chair with his magazines*)

Tom Yes. I meant, in the vacations. I used to take my tent and bicycle off somewhere.

Reg Yes, great that. Get a group of you together . . .

Tom No, no, mostly on my own. Preferred it. I did take someone one year but we didn't really hit it off. He was very—ebullient—I think that's the word. I don't honestly think you can possibly share a small tent for any length of time with someone who's ebullient. I remember he used to lie there in his sleeping-bag, night after night, whistling under his breath. Maddening. It was no good saying anything to him because he had this frightful temper. He couldn't bear it if you criticized him. He'd take it very personally. Practically go berserk. I remember, he once threw my canvas bath on the camp fire. Just because I said something he didn't care for. So I mostly went on my own. Watched for badgers. Impossible to watch badgers with a man like that. Anyway, he failed his finals . . .

Norman snores

Annie Oh, no, we're not going to have to put up with that all evening, are we?

Tom Yes. A whole canvas washstand. On the fire. Ruined it.

Reg If she hadn't flung those biscuits at me we could have had those.

Norman snores

Annie Norman, shut up.

Sarah comes in with the tray of coffee, etc., which she puts on the settee table

Sarah Here we are. Sorry I took so long. I had to rinse the cups again. Someone who shall be nameless had put them away without . . .

Norman snores

Oh, my God, what's that?

Annie Guess who.

Sarah Oh, no, this is too much. I'm not having this. Norman, get up this minute. Norman . . .

Reg Save your breath, he can't hear you. He's bubbling over with dandelion wine.

Sarah Revolting. Well, we can't leave him there, for heaven's sake.

Reg He's all right.

Sarah He is not all right.

Reg He isn't in anybody's way. Leave him alone.

Sarah I am not sitting down to have coffee with that all over the floor.

Reg (*irritated*) Well, what are we supposed to do with him?

Annie (*swiftly*) All right. All right. We'll move him. That's enough. We'll move him. Tom . . .

Tom Um?

Annie Give me a hand.

Reg No. I'll do it. It's all right.

Reg and Tom heave Norman half up by his arms

(*To Sarah*) Now then, madam, would you like him wrapped or will you take him as he is.

Annie (*indicating the window seat*) Put him here.

Annie replaces the bottles and glass on the settee table

Sarah (*watching them deposit Norman*) Absolutely revolting behaviour.
Reg There you go . . .
Annie (*at the coffee*) What's everybody want? White or black?
Sarah No, I'll do it . . .
Annie It's all right.
Sarah No. I'm doing this . . .
Annie I'm already doing it.
Sarah You're not already doing it, I'm doing it.
Annie Oh, don't be so ridiculous, Sarah.
Sarah I'm not being ridiculous. This is your week-end to rest.
Annie Oh, forget that.
Sarah Will you please give me that coffee-pot.
Annie What's the use of . . .
Sarah Annie, will you give me that coffee-pot at once or I shall lose my
temper.
Annie (*thrusting the pot at Sarah*) Oh, go on have the damn thing then.
(*She sits sulkily on the settee*)
Sarah Thank you. (*Recovering her composure*) Now then, everyone. Black
or white?
Reg I should heat it up first. It'll be cold by now.
Sarah (*ignoring him*) Tom?
Tom Um?
Sarah Coffee?
Tom Oh, thanks very much.
Sarah Thank you, Tom. Black or white?
Tom Um? . . . (*He considers*)

A pause

Sarah Annie?
Annie No, thank you.
Sarah Oh, don't be so silly.
Annie None for me, I couldn't drink it.
Sarah Reg?
Tom Black, I think.
Sarah (*shrilly*) I'm asking Reg.
Tom Oh. Sorry.
Reg White.
Sarah Please.
Reg Please.
Sarah At last. White for Reg. Black for Tom. None for Annie.
Tom I think I'll change mine to white on second thoughts.

Sarah gives him a glare. Norman snores

Sarah Is there any way of stopping that noise? (*Holding out two cups to
Tom*) Would you mind, Tom?

Tom takes two cups, gives one to Annie. Annie takes the cup to Reg who sits on the settee. Sarah brings her cup to the settee. Tom gets up, Sarah sits down, Tom tries to, but cannot, so wanders to the settee table and puts sugar in his coffee. He takes two magazines, goes to the low chair and sits. He stirs his coffee noisily and at length. Sarah waits for him to sit before she speaks

Sarah Well now, how would we all like to spend this evening?

A silence

It's not often we're all gathered together like this. I'm sure we can——

Norman snores

—think of something.

A silence

Reg Well, I thought it might be quite fun if we were to have a go at my game, perhaps.

Sarah I'm sure nobody wants to do that.

Reg It'd be quite fun.

Sarah We don't want to waste our evening doing that.

Reg You may not but . . .

Sarah No-one does, don't be so boring.

Reg (*muttering*) I just thought if . . .

Sarah We hardly see each other at all. One of the few occasions we all manage to be together, away from that blessed television and without the children to worry about—wouldn't it be rather nice if for once we could just sit and have a pleasant civilized conversation?

Reg Civilized conversation?

Sarah Yes, why not?

Reg We couldn't have a civilized conversation if we tried. Hark at you just now. You were only pouring the coffee out, there was practically a bloody civil war.

Sarah Well, I'm not wasting my time playing your silly games and that's final.

Silence

Annie I think I'd quite enjoy a game.

Reg Ah!

Sarah What?

Annie And I'm sure Tom would. Wouldn't you, Tom?

Tom Um?

Annie You'd like to play Reg's game, wouldn't you?

Tom (*doubtfully*) Oh . . .

Sarah Of course he doesn't, do you, Tom?

Annie Of course he does, don't you, Tom?

Tom Er . . . (*Looking from woman to woman*) Well . . .

Annie Super. Come on then, Reg.

Reg (*already unpacking the board*) If you're sure you'd like to . . .

Annie Tom . . .

Tom Yes. All right. (*He gets up*)

Reg You going to play, Sarah?
Sarah Well, I suppose if it's a choice between that and sitting on my own . . .
Reg Grand. Get me a chair, Tom.

Tom brings the low chair to Reg, who sits. Tom hovers behind him. Annie pulls the pouffe towards the coffee-table, then sits on the settee. Sarah stands and watches

Sarah I'm not playing for long. I think I'll have an early night.
Reg It's all right, it's quite a quick game.
Sarah I've heard that before.
Tom That one of yours we played before was very complicated.
Reg Ah, you mean my Mountaineering one.
Tom Yes. I seem to remember I kept running out of sherpas.
Reg Ah well, you didn't buy enough sherpa cards to start with. You need the sherpas to carry your oxygen.
Tom Yes, I ran out of that as well. My whole expedition was a total write-off.
Sarah Well, let's play this game, shall we, if we're going to.
Reg Yes, right. Well, sit where you like. Sarah, you go there. And Annie —Tom.

Tom sits on the settee

Sarah (*sitting on the pouffe*) I can't sit here. The board's upside down. I can't read it.
Tom Sit here.
Annie No, she can sit here.
Reg No, it's all right, I'll turn the board round, it's very simple.
Sarah Now you can't read it.
Reg I don't need to read it, I know.
Tom I think I can read it sideways all right.

Sarah now sits opposite Reg, Annie next to Tom

Annie It looks very exciting. (*Picking up a pile of cards*) What are these?
Reg (*anxiously*) No. Don't touch anything.
Annie Sorry.
Reg I'll explain.
Sarah Well, I hope it doesn't take all night.
Reg Right now.
Sarah Don't forget Mother's medicine, will you, Annie?
Annie Five minutes yet.
Reg Right, now. This is the board.
Tom Go slowly, won't you? I'm not awfully quick on these sort of things.
Sarah Hah!
Annie You don't say.
Tom (*a bit nettled for him*) I do my best, I do my best.
Reg Well, just listen, listen carefully. This board represents the street map of a city. Each of these areas marked brown are buildings.

Tom Buildings.

Reg Now, as you see, they are all marked very clearly what they are. These are shops, you see. Greengrocers—outfitters—bank and then along here jewellers—dress shop.

Tom What's this here? Coop. What's a coop?

Reg Co-op.

Tom Oh, co-op. I see. Sorry—reading sideways, you see.

Annie Oh, Tom, for goodness' sake.

Tom All right . . . don't keep on at me, don't keep on at me, there's a good girl.

Annie Well, honestly, you're so slow!

Reg And all these grey areas are the roads.

Sarah Oh, this is far too complicated to learn in one evening.

Reg It's not complicated if you'll listen. Now the object of the game is as follows.

Sarah I mean, it takes an hour just to read the . . .

Reg (*yelling*) Listen!

Norman (*rolling off the window-seat; waking up with a jerk, loudly*) Wah! Wah!

Everyone reacts

Sarah Oh, my God.

Norman (*getting up*) I was having a terrible dream. It was a terrible dream, you've no idea.

Annie You all right, Norman?

Norman Hallo. There was this great big black shape and it was coming after me—like a cloud—only it was making this buzzing noise. (*He demonstrates with a buzzing noise*)

Reg (*over this*) We're having a game at the moment, Norman.

Norman And I was trying to run away from it. But you know how it is in a dream, your feet won't move . . .

Tom I've had that.

Reg Yes, terrible. Now, the object of the game . . .

Norman (*threshing his feet about*) You're running, running, but you're still in the same place. You know you're dreaming but you can't wake up. Terrifying. You came into it, Sarah . . .

Sarah Yes, I think you'd better lie down.

Annie You can use my bed, if you like. I'll make up the spare one later.

Norman stumbles to the window-seat and sits

Sarah No, Norman can sleep on the spare one.

Annie No, it isn't made up.

Sarah Then I'll make it up. (*She rises*)

Reg Oh, come on we're playing a game.

Tom Is this blue thing a road?

Reg No, that's a river.

Tom Ah.

Sarah Are the sheets in the linen cupboard?

Norman rises

Annie Sarah, if you don't mind, I'll deal with it.
Sarah (*going to the door*) There is no need for you to, you're supposed to be having a rest——

Norman blunders into Sarah in the doorway

—Where are you going?
Norman Phone. I've got to phone.
Annie (*indicating the phone*) Well, use this one.
Norman Oh, yes.
Sarah Who are you phoning?
Norman My wife. Ruth. I need to speak to my wife. I demand to speak to my wife . . .

Tom fiddles with the cardboard pieces

Reg Well, phone in another room, there's a good chap . . . (*Knocking Tom's hand from the board*) And don't fiddle with those . . .
Tom Sorry.
Annie (*rising*) He'll have to phone in here. The other one's in Mother's room. God, it's nearly time for her medicine.
Norman I want to speak to Ruth.
Annie (*soothingly, guiding him to the phone*) All right, Norman—here. Sit here. You can phone from here. (*She sits Norman in the easy chair*)
Norman Thank you very much.
Annie Can you manage?
Norman God bless you and keep you.
Sarah Do you think it's wise, him speaking to Ruth?
Annie No idea.
Sarah Probably upset her more than ever.
Annie (*returning to the table*) Probably. (*She sits as before*)
Reg Sarah, are you playing or not?
Sarah (*sitting*) Yes, all right, all right. Let's get it over and done with.
Reg We haven't even started. Now then, the object of the game is as follows. With four players, two of us represent the police, and two of us, the criminals.
Norman (*on the phone*) Hallo . . .
Reg Now, the aim of the criminals——
Norman Ruth? It's me . . .
Reg —is to plan a successful raid——
Norman Me. Norman. I'm at Mother's.
Reg (*with a glare at Norman*) —on any shop they choose. The aim of the police . . .
Norman Your mother's. Of course, your mother's . . .
Reg The aim of the police, obviously, is to stop them.
Norman How the hell can I be at my mother's? She's been dead for ten years . . .
Reg Norman . . .

Norman Well, don't say it in that tone.

Reg Norman . . .

Norman God, can't we even have a—excuse me a minute. (*Covering the mouthpiece, to Reg*) What's that?

Reg Could you keep it down a bit?

Norman Beg your pardon. (*He kneels on the floor and covers his head, then speaks into the phone, softly*) Yes?

Reg Thank you. The aim of the police is to stop the raid and capture the crooks red-handed . . .

Norman (*softly into the phone*) Yes, yes. I know . . .

Reg Is that clear so far?

Sarah Perfectly clear, do get on with it.

Tom Um . . .

Reg I don't think Tom's got it. You followed it so far, Tom?

Tom I think so. Police and crooks, yes. The bit that still worries me is this river. It seems to be running straight through the Co-op. Is that right?

Reg It runs underneath it. Underneath.

Tom Oh, I see. Better not shop in the basement.

Reg (*vastly irritated*) Oh, for heaven's sake . . .

Annie Oh, Tom, do shut up.

Tom (*irritably*) All right. All right . . .

Norman (*loudly, into the phone*) I said, you're a selfish bitch . . . (*As the others turn, covering mouthpiece*) Sorry—sorry. (*Into the phone, softly*) What? Yes—yes.

Sarah Come on, Reg, get on with it.

Reg I am trying to get on with it. Now. The police can spot the criminals as follows. They have three police cars—(*holding up a model car*)—which are these. Police cars can run on the roads but not in the buildings . . .

Sarah That's a relief.

Reg Look, do you mind, do you mind. The police cars can see up to twenty spaces ahead of them and up to four spaces each side. They can't see behind them and they can't see round corners.

Sarah Why can't they see behind them?

Reg Because they can't, that's why.

Tom Motto: don't drive behind a police car.

Norman (*loudly for a second*) Love? What do you know about love . . . (*With an apologetic look at the others, continuing in a lower tone*) Have you ever felt love for a single human being in your life?

Reg The police also have the Chief Superintendent. (*Holding him up*) This chap—he can see up to three spaces ahead of him and three spaces round a corner . . .

Tom Useful chap in a crisis.

Sarah Oh, this is absurd.

Reg What's absurd?

Sarah How can you have a man see three spaces ahead and three round a corner?

Reg Because he's got a very long neck. I don't know, it's a game, woman.

Sarah It's not even realistic.
Reg What's that got to do with it?
Sarah It's not much of a game if it's not even realistic.
Reg What are you talking about? Realistic? (*Leaping up*) What about chess? That's not realistic, is it? What's wrong with chess?
Sarah Oh well, chess . . .
Reg In chess, you've got horses jumping sideways. That's not realistic, is it? Have you ever seen a horse jumping sideways?
Sarah Yes. All right . . .
Reg (*leaping about*) Like this. (*Imitating a "knight's move"*) Jumping like this. Jump, jump-jump. Jump, jump-jump. That's very realistic, I must say.
Sarah You've made your point.
Annie Reg . . .
Reg And bishops walking diagonally. (*Demonstrating again*) You ever seen a bishop walking like this? Well, have you? I'm asking you, have you ever seen a flaming bishop walking like this?
Sarah Reg, will you please sit down and get on with it.
Reg (*sitting, triumphantly*) Well then.
Norman Don't you hang up on me . . . Ruth! Ruth! (*He jangles the receiver up and down*) Hallo? Hallo? What? Who's this? Mother— what are you doing on the line, get off.
Sarah Who's he talking to?
Norman Ruth! Hallo . . . Mother, will you please get off this line.
Annie (*rising*) Oh, my God. He jiggled the receiver . . .
Norman Mother!
Annie He rang the extension bell in Mother's bedroom.
Norman (*into the phone*) Look—would you shut up, both of you, for a minute and let me get a word in . . . Mother, if you don't hang up, I'll come up and sort you out personally.
Annie (*moving to Norman*) Norman . . . (*She tries to take the receiver*)
Norman (*into the phone*) What did you say? (*To Annie*) Go away.
Annie Norman—please . . .
Norman All right, Mother, I've warned you. (*Rising*) I'll come up and wrap it round your neck . . .

Norman bangs the receiver down on the table and strides out

Sarah Norman . . . (*She rises*)
Annie Norman!
Sarah Stop him . . .
Annie Norman!

Annie goes out after Norman

Sarah (*following her*) Well, don't just sit there . . .

Sarah goes out after Annie

Reg I wonder if the bloke who invented Monopoly had this trouble . . .
Tom Very difficult to concentrate. (*He rises, wanders to the phone, picks up the receiver and listens*) Good grief . . .
Reg What's happening?
Tom There's a heck of a rumpus on the extension—yelling their heads off . . . Hallo? Who's that? . . . Ruth? Oh, hallo, Ruth, it's Tom . . . Yes, Tom . . . Fine . . . How are you? . . . Oh . . . Oh . . . Oh, I see . . . Oh, I'm sorry, yes . . . Oh dear . . . Oh dear . . . (*He pulls a face at Reg*) Oh, yes . . . How dreadful . . . Yes . . .

Annie returns, breathless

Annie Tom, Reg, for goodness' sake. Leaving us to cope with Norman. He's practically attacked Mother. He's out of control.
Reg Well, I don't see that . . .
Annie Tom!
Tom What? . . . Just hang on a second, Ruth . . . (*To Annie*) What?
Annie Tom, would you stop standing there looking so useless and do something for once in your life.
Tom What?
Annie I've never met anyone so useless . . .
Tom Now look here. I wish you'd stop going on at me like this. You're damned lucky to have me around, you know.
Annie Oh, really?
Tom Yes, really. Every time anything goes wrong, you seem to take it out on me. First of all, it's your holiday, then it's Norman—well, it's just not on, it really isn't . . .
Annie Um?
Reg Won't somebody play with me, please . . .
Tom The next time you're planning holidays for two, if you want me along, perhaps you'd be good enough to be polite enough to ask me.
Annie You've got a hell of a nerve.
Tom (*pushing Annie aside as he moves to the settee table*) And, anyway, if you want to be seen with me, you'd better smarten yourself up a bit. You're a mess, you know. You look like something that's fallen off a post van.
Annie I beg your pardon?

Norman returns

Norman (*moving straight to the phone, pushing Annie out of his way*) That's settled that.
Annie Norman . . .
Norman (*into the phone*) Ruth? Hallo? . . . She's hung up. Would you believe it, she's hung up on me. (*He replaces the receiver*)
Tom I'm going home, I'm fed up. Just count yourself lucky, I don't belt you one and give you rabies.

Tom strides out to the garden.
   Sarah enters with the blue bed-jacket, which now has two large holes
in it

Sarah Look what you've done. Look what you've done to my bed-jacket.
Norman (*collapsing*) Nobody loves me. Nobody loves me any more.
Annie Norman . . .
Sarah Look at this. Will somebody look at this.
Reg Won't anybody play with me? Please . . .

CURTAIN

ACT II

SCENE 1

The same. Sunday, 9 p.m.

Ruth is standing by the window. Reg sits on the settee making notes about his game

Ruth I shouldn't have wasted my time coming down here. Norman makes these gestures regularly. And every time I fall for them. We've been married for five years, I really ought to know better. As a result of his hysterical phone call last night, I have not been able to do a stroke of work at home today and will probably lose my job tomorrow. When I finally turn up. I almost wish to heavens he'd gone to East Grinstead with Annie, had his week-end and got it over with. Instead of involving everyone else. Mind you, that would be much too simple for Norman. No point in making a gesture unless he has an appreciative crowd to applaud him. (*Looking at her watch*) Too late to drive back now. I think I'll go to bed in a minute.

Reg I'm amazed you two are still together.

Ruth Well. I think other people's marriages are invariably a source of amazement. They usually are to me. I mean, you and Sarah . . . You know, I have found quite often it's the people you look at and say, well, they won't last long who cling on grimly till death. Maybe they're so aware of public opinion, they're determined to prove it wrong. You and Sarah—me and Norman—and Annie and that—Tom man. Though I think Norman's successfully knocked that on the head.

Reg Tom's gone home, then?

Ruth (*looking through the magazines*) I saw him stamping off into the night. Probably the most constructive thing Norman's done for some time. Saved Annie from a fate worse than marriage. A sort of eternal engagement.

Reg I don't know. He's nice enough, Tom.

Ruth Not nice enough for her. Oh—this house! I feel like getting a paintbrush and going over it with red and orange and bright blue. It's like a brown museum. A very dirty brown museum.

Reg Well, you can't expect Annie to . . .

Ruth No, I don't expect Annie to do anything. (*She sits in the easy chair with a magazine*) She's got enough to cope with, with that—evil woman upstairs.

Reg Never got on with Mother either, did you.

Ruth No. She never liked me, I never liked her. Mutual.

Reg We were saying earlier, you and Mother were rather alike.

Ruth (*laughing*) Maybe . . .

Reg I wouldn't say Sarah and I were altogether incompatible. We have differences. I won't try and hide that. We certainly have differences. But you know, six of one . . . She's pretty good with the children. On her good days. Runs the house very well. Better than you or Annie would. Or Mother.

Ruth Of course, she does have the advantage of you running round in circles for her.

Reg That's all right, I don't mind. I prefer being told what to do really. I often think if nobody told me what to do I'd never do anything at all. I remember she went away once for a fortnight. When her father was ill. Took the children with her. Left me on my own in the house. Do you know I felt myself gradually slowing down. At the end of ten days I was hardly moving at all. Extraordinary. It was as if she'd wound me up before she left and now I was running down. I hadn't even got the energy to take the milk in. Sarah reckons I've got some rare tropical disease. Burmese inertia, or something. Anyway, it's better to be calm with Sarah. She's like those toy animals you see in the back windows of cars. Any violent movement from me and she's nodding her head reproachfully for days.

Ruth leaves the magazines by the chair, rises, goes to the settee table and looks at another one

It works all right. Most days.

Annie enters and sits in the easy chair, taking off her shoes

Ruth Who's washing up?

Annie Nobody. I'm not so nobody is. I've done quite enough this weekend. I'm not doing any more.

Ruth Good for you. (*She sits on the settee with the magazine*)

Reg I'll do it in a minute.

Annie No, don't. You did it last night. Somebody else can do it.

Ruth You looking at me?

Annie Or Norman. Or Sarah.

Ruth Ha!

Reg Huh!

Annie I don't know who ever does anything in your house. You and Norman are both as bad as each other.

Ruth continues to read her magazine, holding it a few inches from her nose

Annie What are you doing?

Ruth Trying to read.

Annie You can't read like that. It's resting on your nose.

Ruth I like the smell of newsprint.

Annie Why don't you wear your glasses?

Ruth I can manage, thank you.

Annie If you don't like glasses, you could get contact lenses.
Ruth I tried them. They don't work.
Annie Of course they do.
Ruth They weren't designed for people who share a house with Norman.
Life with him is full of sudden, unexpected eye movements. They kept
falling out. Where the hell did you get all these dreadful magazines?
Reg They're Sarah's.
Ruth Oh. I do beg your pardon.

A pause

Reg Tom's gone home.
Annie Yes.
Reg Ah.

A pause

He'll be back tomorrow, I expect.
Annie I doubt it. Even he has a limit.
Reg Oh, he'll be back.
Ruth It's not altogether our fault if he doesn't come back.
Annie What, after the way everyone's treated him? All right, I know I
haven't been particularly nice either—but that was different. I don't
know why I'm so mean to him sometimes. It's just when you're fond
of someone—you are enough to worry what other people think of them.
You want them to be something they're not capable of being. Which is
very unfair on them really. I mean, he's Tom, isn't he? That's one of
the best things about him. He's always Tom. He never pretends. He
never puts on an act for anybody.
Ruth No, he's always Tom. You're right there.
Annie Well, it's better than living with an emotional big-dipper like
Norman.
Ruth Depends on your tastes, doesn't it?
Annie I know which I'd prefer.
Ruth Then I should stick to it then, if I were you.
Annie All right. I'm sorry. We have been through that. Norman caught
me when I was very depressed. The tale end of that awful Christmas.
He asked me at a time when I hardly knew what I was doing.
Ruth There's no need to explain. He's always been an expert at timing—
whatever else. He proposed to me in a crowded lift. It was total black-
mail. He sounded so appealing he won the sympathy of everyone round
us. Had I been heartless enough to refuse him, they'd have probably
dropped me down the lift shaft. I managed to stall him for three floors
and then the lift man said, "Sorry, folks, nobody gets out till the little lady
says yes". I remember that was the first time I really felt like throttling
Norman.
Reg Very romantic. I proposed to Sarah just out there in the garden, you
know.
Annie Yes, we know. Ruth and I watched you through the window.
Reg You didn't, did you?

Ruth We weren't going to tell him.

Annie Oh, what's it matter now. Sarah was all wobbly and quivering, trying to make up her mind and Ruth kept saying say no, say no.

Reg Thank you.

Annie I must see to Mother in a minute.

Ruth If it's not too tactless a question, how long is she going to remain like that?

Annie Oh, for ever. Well, till she dies.

Ruth Is that what Dr Whatsisname says?

Annie Wickham says there's no reason why she shouldn't last for years. Most of it's psychosomatic. Well, we knew that anyway. She just has no desire to get up. No reason to. So she doesn't. Sad, really. Her whole life was centred round men, wasn't it? When they lost interest in her, she lost interest in herself. I hope I never get like that.

Ruth No danger. Don't worry.

Annie Oh well, yes, I know I'm not quite the *femme fatale* figure but . . .

Ruth (*rising to take another magazine*) I mean that, thank God, you can see a bit further than she ever could. That woman never had a thought in her head in her life. Look at her, lying up there reading those dreadful books.

Annie I'm afraid if I'm here alone with her much longer, I might start to get like her. You know, when I went up to her this afternoon, I had this dress on and a bit of make-up—she was so gleeful. She thought at last her propaganda was beginning to have an effect.

Ruth Well, we'll try and come down more often. If we can. But I've got Norman and Reg has got Mrs Reg and all the little Reggies. You do see.

Annie If you could try.

Ruth Yes, we'll try. Won't we, Reg? (*She sits on the window-seat*)

Reg What? Oh, yes. Bit of a job getting away but I'll see what Sarah can arrange.

Sarah comes in

Sarah Well. (*She sits on the settee*) Nice and quiet for once.

Annie Yes . . .

Sarah What are you doing, Reg?

Reg I'm just . . .

Sarah Oh. Haven't you got anything to do?

Reg I'm doing something.

Sarah Yes—well, don't be too anti-social, will you?

A pause

I've got Norman doing the washing up.

Ruth You've what?

Annie You've really been working the charm.

Sarah No, I just had to ask him. I said would he be very kind since I wasn't feeling really up to it and—he was perfectly agreeable.

Ruth You must pass on the secret. Everything that can fall to bits in our house has done so. All the doorknobs come off in your hand. None of the cupboards open, three of the windows are stuck, the fridge needs a plug and on wet days, we have to climb out of the front-room window to go to work because the front door warps when it rains. I could probably do it myself but I'm damned if I'm going to.

Sarah If you don't mind my saying so, I think you just handle Norman wrongly. If you ask him nicely, he's very willing and helpful.

Annie That's good coming from you. You always say he's impossible.

Sarah I think we underestimate Norman.

Annie What have you been up to out there?

Sarah What do you mean?

Ruth Better change the subject.

Sarah I don't know what you mean,

Norman enters with the salad basket

Norman Excuse me.

Reg Hey hey. The domestic man.

Norman Liberated to the kitchen.

Annie Just sling it on top of the cupboard.

Norman Sling it, right.

Annie Just gently, Norman, don't get carried away.

Norman Right-ho, Chief.

Norman salutes and goes

Ruth What a revolting sight. What have you done with the slob I married.

Annie She's house-trained him at last.

Ruth That I doubt. (*Rising*) Well, on that awful picture I'm going to bed. Which room was Norman untidying last night?

Annie The spare room. Reg's old one.

Ruth Right. Tell Norman, if he wants to join me he may. But I'd prefer it if he came on his own. (*Waving her magazine at Sarah*) May I borrow this to read?

Sarah Of course.

Ruth It's so gruesome, it should frighten me to sleep. Good night, all.

Annie Do you want a call in the morning?

Ruth If you sleep with Norman, you wake at dawn. Be warned.

Ruth goes out

Sarah Good night.

Reg 'Night.

Annie 'Night. (*She looks at one of the magazines*)

Sarah Personally, I think if she showed Norman a little more kindness and encouragement she might find him a little less difficult . . .

Annie Well, don't let one success go to your head.

Sarah Let's face it, Ruth's always had difficulty getting on with anybody. Most of the time she doesn't try.

Unseen by Sarah, Ruth returns for her handbag

I'm sure Norman's difficult to live with. I've no doubt. But any man who had to live with Ruth for any length of time . . .

Reg clears his throat

No, I mean honestly I . . . (*She tails off as she sees Ruth*)
Ruth Good night.

Ruth goes out

Sarah (*in an undertone*) She did that deliberately.
Reg (*rising*) Well, I think I'll follow on. Do you mind if I go in the bathroom first?
Sarah No.
Reg Got to drive in the morning. Get an early night.
Sarah Would you switch on the blanket, dear?
Reg Right. Do you want a bottle?
Sarah No, it's too mild for a bottle. I just want the chill off the sheets. They seemed a little damp last night.
Reg Right. (*He goes to peck Sarah on the cheek. They bump noses*) See you up there then.
Sarah All right.
Annie 'Night, Reg.

Reg goes out

Sarah I don't know when we'll get down here again. I think we're very booked up between now and Christmas.
Annie Oh well, if you can. You know . . .
Sarah It would be so much easier if we could bring the children . . .
Annie Well, do, there's room for them.
Sarah Oh, no. They'd disturb Mother.
Annie She wouldn't mind. She'd like to see them.
Sarah No. I don't think so, really. They're very noisy. We'll all come down again at Christmas, if Mother's any better. (*Pause*) I hope Tom isn't too upset.
Annie Don't know.
Sarah I expect he'll be back.
Annie Expect so.
Sarah I mean, he must realize it wasn't anything serious between you and Norman.
Annie Maybe, maybe.
Sarah I mean, as Norman says, it was just an idiotic idea of his.
Annie Did he say that?
Sarah Yes, he was saying in the kitchen, it was nothing in the least serious.

He just thought you looked a bit tired and fed up and needed a change. Act of charity, really.

Annie Oh. Is that what he said?

Sarah Nothing for Tom to get jealous about.

Annie No.

Sarah Why don't you go up to bed, too. You're looking very washed out.

Annie I have to see to Mother first.

Sarah I'll tell you what, I'll see to Mother. You get an early night for once.

Annie All right. You may have to read to her, I warn you.

Sarah I don't mind. I'll read to her.

Annie You wait till you see what she reads.

Sarah (*hustling her along*) All right then, come on, up you go.

Annie Yes, I'm going. (*She remains sitting, looking at the magazine*)

Sarah What's Mother due for, now?

Annie (*consulting her watch*) Er—nine-thirty. Two green ones and one pink if she'll swallow it. Try and persuade her to. She's got a thing about the pink ones for some reason. She says they make her giddy.

Sarah (*hurrying to the door*) Two green, one pink. (*Turning*) Coming?

Annie Yes. All right. I'm coming . . .

Sarah (*hovers for a second, then reluctantly gives up*) Well. Don't stay down too long. (*She switches out the pendant, depriving Annie of most of her reading light*) Good night.

Annie 'Night. (*She stands indeterminate. She wanders to the window and looks out unhappily*) Oh. Hell . . . (*She goes to the bookcase*) Read it—read it—read it—read it . . . (*She goes to the pile of magazines and starts to select one*)

Norman comes in with a saucepan

Norman Er—oh.

Annie On the wall. Over the draining-board, there's a hook.

Norman A hook. Right. Everyone gone to bed?

Annie Yes.

Norman It's too bad, you know, I'm slaving away out there. Ruth gone to bed?

Annie Yes. She said you're welcome to join her.

Norman Oh.

Annie Which I think is very reasonable of her, really. I'm not sure I'd be as generous.

Norman You've really gone off me, haven't you?

Annie Just a bit, Norman, yes.

Norman What can I do?

Annie I think we don't talk about it. I think we just keep out of each other's way. You'll be going home tomorrow morning then we can forget all about it.

Norman I was going to take you away, you know.

Annie I don't want to talk about it, Norman.

Norman I would have done. I was ready. I had it all planned. It was you. You said . . .

Annie (*going to pick up her shoes*) Good night, Norman. (*She goes to the door*)

Norman Annie. Just a second, please . . .

Annie (*turning*) Good night.

Norman I didn't mean to mess it up for you and Tom, I really didn't.

Annie That's all right. You didn't.

Norman But he's gone off.

Annie I did that myself.

Norman Then why are you blaming me for it?

Annie Because as I say, Norman, I feel like I've been taking part in one of Reg's games. Only in this case, you and Ruth are making up all the rules as you go along.

Norman What's Ruth got to do with it? She would never have known.

Annie Until you phoned her.

Norman I only phoned her when you changed your mind. I got drunk. I was unhappy. Oh, Annie, I wanted this week-end for you. I wanted it to be . . .

Annie An act of charity.

Norman What?

Annie Nor do I like you discussing me in the kitchen with Sarah. Making out you'd taken pity on me, for God's sake.

Norman Who told you that?

Annie Sarah told me. If you want a secret kept don't tell Sarah in future.

Norman I only said that to calm her down. You know what Sarah's like. Gets all het up . . .

Annie I'm going to have an early night, Norman, I'm off.

Norman I was really looking forward to our week-end, you know.

Annie So was I.

Norman Sorry.

Annie Not all your fault.

Norman Another time, eh?

Annie Not on your life.

Norman (*sitting on the settee arm*) Oh. If I booked early enough, I could perhaps get us into Hastings next year.

Annie Oh, Norman.

Norman I mean, not that there's anything wrong with East Grinstead but . . .

Annie Good night.

Norman Annie. (*He falls back on the settee, looking up at her*)

Annie (*coming back into the room*) What?

Norman Can I kiss you good night?

Annie No.

Norman Can I kiss you good-bye then? Please.

Annie Norman. You are definitely evil.

Norman I love you.

Annie No.

Norman Kiss?

Annie Not until you take that back.

Norman What?

Annie That you love me. It's not true. Don't say it.

Norman All right. I don't love you. Can I have a kiss, please?

Annie Okay. Come on.

Norman hesitates

   Come and get it if you want it.

Norman Don't say it like that.

Annie Well, how am I supposed to say it?

Norman Well. Nicely. Like you did at Christmas.

Annie All right. Kiss me, Norman.

Norman No.

Annie What?

Norman Come over here, first. On our rug.

Annie Now don't you start that.

Norman No, no. Just a kiss. Promise.

Annie I don't trust you.

Norman Look, I'm holding a saucepan.

Annie What's that got to do with it?

Norman I've only got one hand.

Annie I seem to remember you can do a lot with one hand.

Norman Promise.

Annie Just one kiss.

Norman Yes.

Annie (*moving to him*) Good night and good-bye, Norman.

They kiss. A little longer than Annie had planned. Norman's saucepan flails in the air

   Sarah enters. She carries a pill bottle. She sees Annie and Norman. She pauses for a second and then, banging down the bottle, advances furiously and swiftly across the room

Norman sees Sarah over Annie's shoulder and tries to pull out of the kiss, with a muffled warning. He is too late. Sarah grabs Annie by the shoulder and shoves her away from Norman

Sarah You deceitful little whore. Get upstairs. Get up to bed this instant.

Annie (*amazed*) Who do you think you're talking to?

Sarah (*shoving Annie again*) Get upstairs! Go on . . .

Annie And, please, I do not like being pushed around.

Sarah I will push you around just as much as I . . .

Annie You will not, you know.

Sarah (*pushing Annie again*) Get upstairs, do you hear me? Get upstairs.

Annie I warn you, Sarah, you push me once more, I'll slap your stupid face.

Norman I say . . .

Annie And you can shut up, too, Norman
Sarah You're a really nasty piece of work, aren't you? All that innocent little girl act. You're just a tart like your Mother.
Annie Sarah, I will not have you talking about my Mother like that.
Sarah Dirty little slut.
Annie If you call me any more names . . .
Sarah Slut, slut.
Annie (*raising a rather impressive looking fist*) You asked for it.

Annie advances menacingly on Sarah. Sarah retreats

Sarah Don't you come near me. Don't you dare threaten me.
Annie Then take it back.

Ruth enters. She is now dressed only in an old dressing-gown, Norman's

Ruth stands for a moment bemused, taking in the scene, Annie and Sarah about to come to blows and Norman beginning to enjoy every minute of it

Sarah I will not take it back. You're a tart and a slut.
Annie Don't you call me that, you frustrated bitch.
Sarah Keep away. Keep away . . .
Annie I'll ring your stupid neck.
Ruth (*thundering*) Annie! Sarah! That's enough.

A silence

All right, that's enough.
Sarah (*quite hysterical*) She has no right to say that to me.
Ruth (*sharply*) I said that's enough. Good night, Sarah.
Sarah If you'd seen what she . . .
Ruth Good night, Sarah.

Sarah goes to the door, gives a last indignant glare back into the room and goes out

Good night, Annie.
Annie (*taking her shoes and going slowly to the door*) Good night.
Norman (*lamely*) 'Night.

Annie goes out

A very long silence. Ruth seems lost for words. She opens her mouth to speak to Norman, then does not. She walks up and down. She opens her mouth to speak to him again. She cannot. She walks about some more

Ruth (*finally*) Do you ever realize, Norman, the number of times in a day I could lose my temper with you and don't?

Norman continues to study his toes and the saucepan

I usually manage by some supreme effort of will to control it. Well,

this time, I'm sorry, I'm quite unable to. (*Moving to him*) You under-
stand what I'm saying, Norman? I am simply bloody livid. (*She slaps his face*)

Norman Ow.

Ruth How could you, Norman, how could you do it? Don't you think it
was bad enough for me at Christmas to lie there ill in bed? Knowing you
were down here playing around with not one woman, but two.

Norman (*muttering*) I wasn't playing with two.

Ruth Why do you do it? Don't you have any feeling for me?

Norman I don't know, I'm just . . .

Ruth Just what?

Norman I'm just magnetic or something.

Ruth You are not magnetic, Norman. Not at all. You are odious. You
are deceitful, odious, conceited, self-centred, selfish, inconsiderate and
shallow.

Norman I'm not shallow.

Ruth Have you anything to say at all? Anything?

Norman That's my dressing-gown, isn't it?

Ruth moves around agitatedly for a second

Ruth I don't know what to say. I just don't know what to say . . . And stop
looking like that, for heaven's sake.

Norman Like what?

Ruth Giving me that awful doggie look of yours. It may work wonders
with those two but it does nothing for me. I've seen it far too much.

*Ruth sits away from him, on the settee. Norman wanders unhappily, and
puts the saucepan on the settee table*

Well, I think this is it, don't you? I think this is where we say thank you
very much, good-bye. On top of everything else you've made me look
a complete fool . . . (*Peering round*) Where have you gone, I can't see
you?

Norman Over here.

Ruth Oh. No, I think you're just contemptible.

Norman (*edging towards her and finally touching her hand*) I'm sorry.

Ruth Don't.

Norman I am.

Ruth Let go of my hand.

Norman I am.

Ruth Will you let go of my hand.

Norman Why?

Ruth Because I don't want you touching me.

Norman Oh. (*He wanders away*) So you want me to go, do you?

Ruth I think it's the only thing left.

Norman For you.

Ruth And for you. You're obviouly not made to be married. You never
were. Stupid of me to try and make you behave like a husband in the

first place. You'd be much happier if you were perfectly free, flitting from woman to woman as the mood takes you.

Norman I don't do that.

Ruth You'd like to.

Norman I know the real reason.

Ruth Reason for what?

Norman Why you want to get rid of me. Because I interfere with your work. That's why you'd like to get rid of me.

Ruth Talk about turning the conversation. You really are the limit.

Norman Well . . .

Ruth That isn't true, either.

Norman Which comes first then? Which comes first? Work or me?

Ruth You do. Did.

Norman Work or me?

Ruth I've said, you.

Norman Work or me?

Ruth I'm not going on with this.

Norman You can't, can you? You know it's not true.

Ruth We'll talk about this in the morning. You can sleep down here.

Norman Where?

Ruth I don't know. In a chair. You're certainly not coming up with me. I refuse to be number three in a night.

Norman Nothing happened, you know. They both just started fighting. I was just saying good night to Annie and then Sarah attacked her.

Ruth Oh, yes, really? How interesting. That sounds so terribly likely.

Norman It's true. You're the only one, Ruth. You know that.

Ruth I certainly don't.

Norman Well, you should know that. You should know me by now. I mean, this whole week-end was—for you.

Ruth For me? What do you mean it was for me?

Norman It was a gesture for you.

Ruth Really.

Norman Of course it was. You know that.

Ruth (*studying him*) I don't think you're any of those things I said you were. You're just stupid.

Norman Possibly.

Ruth You just don't think. You want locking up. All right, then.

Norman What?

Ruth Come on. Come upstairs if you're coming. (*Moving to the door*) I must be half-witted but still . . . (*She waits*) Come on.

Norman (*moving to the rug and smiling*) Here a minute.

Ruth What?

Norman Just come here a second.

Ruth (*moving in slightly*) What for?

Norman Please . . .

Ruth (*moving in further*) Why?

Norman (*beckoning her in*) Bit closer—closer—that's it.

Ruth Now, I'm not in the mood for games, Norman.

Norman No. That's it. (*He draws her to him and kisses her*) I love you.
Ruth You really are the most . . .

Norman starts to pull her down on to the rug

   What are you doing?
Norman I suddenly had this wonderful idea.
Ruth What?
Norman On the rug. Come on, on the rug.
Ruth What?
Norman On the rug. Come on.
Ruth Norman, no . . .
Norman It's nice on the rug—come on, on the rug.
Ruth Norman—really.

He kisses her

Norman There. Isn't it nice on the rug?
Ruth Norman . . .
Norman Oh, Ruth . . .

They kiss and roll over

Ruth It's nice on the rug.
Norman I told you it was. It can be our rug.
Ruth Norman . . .

The lights fade as they enjoy the rug and each other

CURTAIN

SCENE 2

The same. Monday, 8 a.m.

Ruth and Norman are now rolled up in the rug asleep. Norman's jacket is a pillow. Reg enters without seeing them. He carries two suitcases. He places one on the floor, puts the other on the table and starts packing away his game. Ruth flings out her arm and hits Reg's leg. Reg jumps. He turns and sees her

Reg Flipping heck!
Ruth Reg . . . ? (*Realizing where she is*) Oh, my God. Norman. Norman, wake up, you fool . . .
Norman (*instantly awake*) What—what—what—morning—what?
Ruth Norman . . .
Norman Oh—oh, God. Hallo, Reg. Ruth, we've overslept. (*He starts to try to get up*)
Ruth (*yelling*) Don't unroll the rug yet. Wait a minute.
Norman Sorry. Oh yes . . .

Ruth and Norman wriggle about under the rug adjusting their dress

Ruth (*as they do so*) You don't really have to stand there gaping, do you, Reg?

Reg Oh, no. Sorry, no. 'Morning. (*He continues packing up the game*)

Ruth (*satisfied that her dressing-gown is again covering her*) All right.

Norman Right.

They unroll from the rug

Ruth Honestly. (*She gets up*) You fool, Norman. Why didn't you wake up? Please, Reg, don't say anything to anyone, will you? I beg you. I'll never live it down.

Reg No—no . . .

Ruth Honestly, Norman, you fool. Why didn't you wake up?

Ruth goes out

Norman smiles amiably at Reg

Reg I take it you two have patched up your little differences?

Norman My wife and I have come to an agreement.

Reg Good.

Norman (*getting up*) Lovely morning—oooh! She's been lying on my arm. Oooh, oooh, oooh. (*He finds his apron backwards and twists it round*) Wouldn't tell anybody about this. (*He straightens the rug*)

Reg No.

Norman Otherwise they'll all want to do it.

Reg Don't think I fancy it. Prefer my bed. Despite the wife. (*He laughs*)

Norman You're off then?

Reg She seems to be hurrying me along for some reason, yes. What was the matter with her last night, do you know?

Norman Who?

Reg Sarah. She came to bed shaking. I've never seen her so bad. I mean, literally shaking. The whole bed was vibrating for hours. Like sleeping on top of a spin dryer.

Norman It must have been the over-excitement.

Reg What over-excitement?

Norman No idea.

Reg Not much of that this week-end was there? Well, the old arguments but that's usual. I must say, on the whole, I've enjoyed the rest.

Norman Yes. Good to get out to the countryside occasionally.

Reg You're right there.

Sarah comes in with a bag

Sarah Reg, have you brought those . . . ? Ah, yes—oh. (*She sees Norman*)

Norman 'Morning.

Sarah (*coolly*) Good morning. (*To Reg*) What are you doing?

Reg Just packing. Just packing.

Sarah (*collecting up the magazines*) Oh, we're not lugging that all the way home with us again, are we?
Reg I'm not leaving it here. This took me months to make.

Norman wanders to the door

Sarah We're never going to have time for it, Reg.
Reg It's all right, I think I've adapted it now so I can play on my own.
Sarah (*piling the magazines on the settee table*) And you promised to take these magazines up to Mother.
Reg I will. I'm going to. I'll have my breakfast first.
Sarah (*picking up the saucepan*) And we can't waste too much time over that, either. (*Coldly to Norman, who is blocking the way out*) Excuse me, please.

Sarah goes out

Reg What's the hurry? We're in a hurry. I don't think she's forgiven you yet, by the look of it.
Norman No.
Reg No. Very cool. Got a long memory has Sarah. It'll be a few months before you're back in favour.
Norman Ah well. I'll try and win her round.
Reg No chance. You'll be told when you're forgiven and not before. She doesn't talk to me for days on end sometimes. Amazing how she remembers to keep it up. I mean, if I have a row in the morning, when I come home in the evening I've forgotten all about it. Until I open the front door. Then it hits you straightaway. Atmosphere like a rolling-pin. Know what I mean? She's got great emotional stamina, my wife.
Norman So have I.
Reg You'll need it. Good luck.

Norman goes out

Reg, alone, whistles a tune, wanders to the centre of the room, looks at the rug and laughs. He wanders to the window and stares out

Reg Oh, hallo. What are you doing out there?

Tom comes in from the garden rather tentatively

Tom Ah . . .
Reg What were you doing hiding out there? Thought you were a cat burglar. (*He laughs*)
Tom No. Er—thought I'd just look in, you know. I was on my way to—somewhere—and I thought I'd look in.
Reg Come in. (*He goes to the magazine pile and tidies it*)
Tom Thank you.

Tom picks up a magazine, Reg puts it back, several times

Reg Nice day again.
Tom Um?
Reg Lovely.
Tom I'm afraid I flew off the handle last night.
Reg Oh, don't worry.
Tom I shouldn't think I'll be very welcome here today.
Reg Why ever not? Don't worry . . .
Tom I didn't sleep at all. Turning it over in my mind, you know. I mean, let's face it. What claim have I got to Annie? None at all. Why should I kick up a fuss—if somebody else . . .
Reg It's natural. Human nature.
Tom I shouldn't have blown my top.
Reg I don't honestly think a lot of people noticed.
Tom Really?
Reg No.
Tom I was very boorish.
Reg Well . . .

Annie comes in dressed as in Act I, Scene 1

Annie Oh. Hallo.
Tom Hallo.
Annie There's some tea and stuff in there, if you want it, Reg.
Reg Oh, right-ho. Wonderful.
Annie Not a lot but . . .
Reg Right. (*Pause*) I think I'll take these up to Mother. Before I forget. Otherwise Sarah'll be on to me again. Excuse me.

Reg picks up the pile of magazines and goes out

Tom Yes. I must be getting along, I think. I was just . . .
Annie Tom.
Tom Yes.
Annie Stay a minute.
Tom All right. (*He looks at his watch*) Yes, fine. (*He looks at his watch again*) Fine. I came to apologize really.
Annie What for?
Tom Well, for—yesterday—losing my temper and—general things.
Annie No need to apologize.
Tom No, I know there isn't. Everyone keeps telling me that. But I think an apology's due. I came to give it. To you.
Annie Thank you.
Tom Well. (*He looks at his watch*) Well . . .
Annie Do you want a cup of tea before you go?
Tom Oh. If there's one going. Won't say no. Didn't feel like breakfast when I got up. Felt a bit sick actually, but—er . . .
Annie Come on then.
Tom You think they'll—er—welcome me in there?

Annie Why ever not? Come on. (*She starts to lead Tom out*)

> *Ruth enters as Tom and Annie reach the door. She is now dressed, and is carrying Norman's case, jacket, overcoat and woolly cap. The medals have been removed from the jacket*

Tom Oh, Ruth, I—er ...

Ruth Oh hallo, Tom, good morning. You're bright and early. (*She puts the case by the easy chair*)

Tom Ruth, I ...

Ruth Mmm? (*She puts the clothes over the back of the easy chair*)

Tom I—er—nothing.

Ruth What's wrong?

Annie Nothing's wrong. Come on.

Tom Right.

> *Norman enters as Tom and Annie go out*

Norman Hallo. Good morning, Mr Vet. (*He slaps Tom on the back*)

> *Tom and Annie go out*

You're dressed.

Ruth (*sitting on the settee*) I wasn't going home in your dressing-gown. I've come up in a rash. I think it was from that rug.

Norman Really? That's unusual.

Ruth What do you mean unusual? Do you make a habit of rolling people on the rug?

Norman No.

Ruth No?

Norman No. You look fabulous this morning.

Ruth I look simply dreadful. I couldn't see my face. I haven't had a bath. I feel terrible.

Norman I love that dress. It's great.

Ruth It's the same one I had on yesterday.

Norman Is it?

Ruth I only brought one with me. I didn't plan to spend the night in the hearth. I suppose you want me to drive you home now?

Norman Yes, please.

Ruth I have to go to work.

Norman You'll have to go home first, you can't go to work like that. You look a dreadful mess.

Ruth Yes. You're supposed to be at work, too.

Norman I was taken ill, haven't you heard?

Ruth I'm amazed they keep you on.

Norman I'm a very good librarian, that's why. I know where all the dirty bits are in all the books.

Ruth We'd better say good-bye.

Norman No breakfast.

Ruth You can get something at home. If there is anything—which I doubt.

Norman What would you say—if I asked you a favour?

Ruth What sort of favour?

Norman Would you take the day off and stay at home?

Ruth No.

Norman Not even with me?

Ruth Especially not with you.

Norman Please.

Ruth Norman, I am doing a full-time job. I just can't . . .

Norman I could ring up for you. I could say you were ill.

Ruth No.

Norman Oh, why can't you be ill for once? Go on, be ill. I know. I'll pretend I'm the doctor. I'll say, I am phoning up on behalf of Mrs Norman Dewers. I have just examined this woman on the rug. She has an ugly rash and in my opinion, she's in great need of some attention. Attention from who, you may ask. (*He leaps to Ruth and sits on the settee*)

Ruth Norman . . .

Norman Kiss.

Ruth Norman. (*She kisses him*)

Norman Are you happy?

Ruth What?

Norman Do I make you happy at all?

Ruth Well . . .

Norman Say you're happy.

Ruth Why? Is it important?

Norman Yes. I want you to be happy. I want everyone to be happy. I want to make everyone happy. It's my mission in life . . .

Ruth Yes, all right, Norman. Well, let's not worry about other people too much, just concentrate on making me happy, will you? The other people will have to try to be happy without you, won't they?

Norman But you are happy?

Ruth Yes. I'm fairly happy.

Norman And you might possibly—feel ill—if you drove very fast all the way home and—somebody made you a cup of tea and—made the bed and—ran you a bath and—put in the bath salts and . . .

Ruth Yes. I might.

Norman How are you feeling?

Ruth Dreadful.

Norman (*with a great cry of joy*) Ha-ha! (*He grabs her*)

Reg enters with a bunch of flowers in tissue. He puts them on the settee table

Reg Oh, blimey, they're at it again.

Sarah and Annie come in

Ruth breaks from Norman

Sarah Well, I think we're ready to go.
Reg One piece of toast. One piece of toast. How can I drive on one piece of toast.

Norman puts on his jacket

Annie Have you got everything?
Sarah I think so. Did you take our sponge bag out of the bathroom, Reg?
Reg Yes, yes, yes.
Ruth Well, I'm going to see if I can start the car.
Norman Right. (*He starts to put on his mac and hat*)
Ruth Oh, Norman, you don't have to put all that on.
Norman I prefer to travel incognito.
Ruth You've still got that suit on. It isn't even yours.
Norman Oh, yes. Can I borrow this, please?
Annie Well, Father doesn't need it any more. You might as well.
Ruth It doesn't even fit him.
Norman I could do with a new executive suit.
Ruth Come on. (*To Sarah, Reg and Annie in turn*) Good-bye. Good-bye. Good-bye.
Annie 'Bye, Ruth.
Reg 'Bye, 'bye.
Sarah Good-bye.
Ruth (*going*) I'm in the car. I'm leaving in ten seconds.

Ruth exits to the garden

Norman All right. All right. (*To Annie*) Good-bye, Annie. Thank you and . . .
Annie (*fairly cool*) Good-bye, Norman.
Norman Reg.
Reg So long.
Norman Sarah. (*He shakes Sarah's hand*)
Sarah (*warmly*) Good-bye, Norman. Have a good journey. See you at Christmas, I hope.
Norman Like the mistletoe, I shall be here.
Ruth (*off*) Norman!
Norman Bag. Where's my bag?
Reg (*pointing*) That it?

Norman goes for his case

Ruth (*off*) Norman!
Sarah (*going to the door and calling*) He's just coming, Ruth, he's just coming.

Reg She's forgiven you very quickly, hasn't she?
Norman You think so?
Reg What did you say to her?
Norman Nothing. I just cheered her up a bit. 'Bye 'bye. Good-bye, Annie Good-bye, Sarah.
Ruth (*off*) Norman, I have left.
Norman All right, all right, I'm coming.

Norman goes, his hand brushing Sarah's as he passes her

Reg Well. Nice to see him, but I'm glad it's only twice a year.
Sarah Yes, I think it's time we were... Good-bye, Annie. (*She pecks Annie's cheek*) Take care, won't you?
Annie And you. Have a good journey.
Reg Thank you.
Annie You won't mind if I don't come and see you off, will you? I must get back to Tom. He's sitting there waiting. He's decided he'd like breakfast after all.
Sarah Oh, yes, you go back to Tom.
Reg Annie, I told him not to worry about this week-end. I did right, did I? To tell him that?
Annie Yes.
Reg Hope everything works out.
Annie Expect so.
Sarah (*at the window*) Norman's having to push that car of theirs.
Reg (*to Annie*) Want a tip? Take Tom out there. Sit him under the tree. Good place to make a proposal out there.
Annie It worked for you.
Reg Yes.
Annie I'll try it. One of these days. 'Bye, 'bye.
Sarah Good-bye, Annie dear.
Reg 'Bye, love.

Annie goes out to the house

Sarah Oh, I am fond of this garden. Even though it's overgrown. Oh, just look at Norman. What does he think he's doing. (*She laughs*)
Reg Could do with a lot of work. I thought they were still paying someone to look after it. That old man. He's worse than useless. No-one keeps an eye on him. So he doesn't do a stroke.
Sarah As long as the sun's shining, I'm happy.
Reg Are you? (*He picks up the cases*)

Sarah stands smiling serenely

You're very cheerful.
Sarah Why shouldn't I be?
Reg No. No reason. Carry on.
Sarah Can you manage those?

Reg Just about.

Pause

Sarah I wonder what Bournemouth would be like at this time of year?
Reg Bournemouth?
Sarah Yes.
Reg What made you suddenly think of Bournemouth?
Sarah It just occurred to me.
Reg You don't want to go to Bournemouth, do you?
Sarah Not now . . .
Reg I thought we were going home.
Sarah Not now. Sometime. I think I'd rather fancy it. Next year—perhaps.
Reg All right. I'll take you. If it'll make you happy.
Sarah No, you don't need to bother. I could go on my own easily.
Reg On your own?
Sarah Leave you in peace for a bit. Just for the week-end. Be rather nice to get away. For a week-end . . .
Reg Don't know why you want to go to Bournemouth. Why Bournemouth? Why not make it Brighton? Or Worthing? (*Sarah goes out to the garden, taking the bunch of flowers*) Or Reigate, for that matter? Or East Grinst . . . (*He pauses. An awful thought*) Oh, my God. Sarah! Wait for me, love. Sarah . . .

Reg hurries out with his cases

CURTAIN

FURNITURE AND PROPERTY LIST

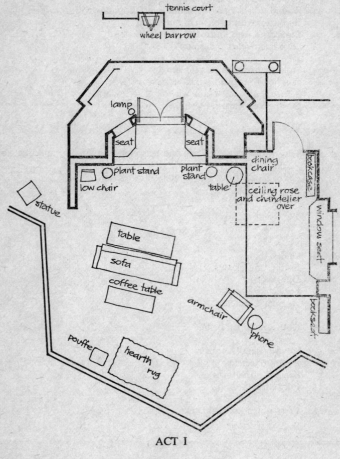

ACT I

SCENE 1

On stage: Pouffe
Settee with antimacassar and 2 cushions
Easy chair matching settee
Brown fur hearth rug
Coffee-table

Low round table. *On it:* telephone, notepad, pencil
Settee table. *On it:* large suitcase containing blue bed-jacket in tissue
    paper, game board and pieces, one loose piece, dressing. *Under*
    table: waste-paper basket
Dining chair
Low chair
Plant stand with plant
Stand with table lamp. *In front of it:* suitcase
Round table. *Under it:* wind-up gramophone with record in place
Bookcase with books. *On top:* lamp
In garden: wheelbarrow
On window-seat: 3 cushions

Off stage: Small battered suitcase (**Norman**)
               Bundle of magazines tied with string (**Reg**)
               3 bottles of home-made wine, 3 glasses, corkscrew (**Annie**)
               Dustpan and brush (**Annie**)

SCENE 2

Off stage: Tray with 4 cups, saucers and teaspoons, coffee-pot, milk jug, sugar
                 basin (**Sarah**)
               Bed-jacket with two large holes in it (**Sarah**)

ACT II

SCENE 1

Strike: Coffee things
               Bottles and glasses
               Dining chair
               Low chair
               Norman's suitcase

Set: Ruth's handbag behind settee

Off stage: Salad basket (**Norman**)
               Apron (**Norman**)
               Saucepan (**Norman**)
               Pill bottle (**Sarah**)

Personal: **Reg:** notebook and pencil

SCENE 2

Off stage: 2 suitcases (**Reg**)
               Norman's suitcase, mac, hat and suit jacket (**Ruth**)
               Bunch of roses in tissue paper (**Sarah**)

Personal: Wrist watch for **Sarah, Annie, Ruth, Reg, Tom**
               Sarah: handbag with handkerchief and compact
               Ruth: handbag with handkerchief and compact

LIGHTING PLOT

Property fittings required: Pendant, 2 table lamps, garden light
Interior. A living-room. The same scene throughout

ACT I, SCENE 1. Evening

To open: Effect of early summer evening light

No cues

ACT I, SCENE 2. Evening

To open: Effect of summer evening—2 hours later than above but still daylight

Cue 1   **Tom** exits to garden   (Page 17)
             Snap on garden light

ACT II, SCENE 1. Late evening

To open: All practicals on

Cue 2   **Sarah** switches off pendant   (Page 34)
             *Snap off pendant and covering spots, including those over easy
               chair*

Cue 3   **Ruth:** "Norman . . ."   (Page 40)
             Fade to Black-Out

ACT II, SCENE 2 Morning

To open: Effect of bright morning sunshine

No cues

EFFECTS PLOT

ACT I

SCENE 1

Cue 1   **Norman** puts on record   (Page 14)
         Music: Richard Tauber singing "Girls were made to Love
             and Kiss"—continue till Curtain

SCENE 2

No cues

ACT II

SCENE 1

Cue 2   **Ruth:** "Norman . . ."   (Page 40)
         Music: Tauber record as above, as Lights fade

SCENE 2

No cues